Happy Birthday Dolly
Sharing Happiness

written by
Lynn C. Skinner

illustrated by
Ingrid Dohm

Happy Birthday Dolly
Copyright © 2020 by Lynn C. Skinner. All rights reserved.

No part of this publication may be reproduced, stored in a retrieval system or transmitted in any way by any means, electronic, mechanical, photocopy, recording or otherwise without the prior permission of the author except as provided by USA copyright law.

Published by Lynn C. Skinner
PO Box 34 | Alley, Georgia 30410 USA
Cover and Layout Design by Christina Hicks Creative

Published in the United States of America
softcover isbn: 978-1-7336531-2-1
ebook isbn: 978-1-7336531-3-8

This book belongs to:

_____

This book is dedicated to Dolly who shares happiness every day.

ACKNOWLEDGMENT

My thanks to Dolly's mother for allowing the author and illustrator to share her story.

When Dolly was born, her parents were so happy. She was a beautiful baby and every member of the family enjoyed holding and rocking her.

When Dolly was young, she developed problems with her bones and she had to wear leg braces. Dolly's eyes also needed thick glasses, but Dolly always smiled.

When she began to talk, Dolly could not say the consonants so she developed her own speech. Her family soon learned all her sounds. Dolly's favorite words were "I ov u" (I love you) and "Og uice ease" (orange juice please.)

As Dolly grew, she learned to say, "I ant a ug." (I want a hug). Dolly was very lovable.

Through the years, Dolly had many operations but she maintained her humorous side. She often put her shoes on the wrong feet and laughed. Then she corrected them.

One of her favorite outings was a trip to the zoo to watch the monkeys.

As Dolly grew older, her family had an idea. They decided to give her a surprise birthday party. It was called Celebrating Dolly.

The invitations were mailed. The room was decorated with balloons and flowers.

Dolly's favorite foods were prepared, including a chocolate fountain with bowls of marshmallows.

It was time for the party. Dolly arrived wearing her new party dress.

When Dolly entered the room, her favorite music was playing. Even though she couldn't really sing, she joyfully sang from her heart.

When the party guests said good-bye, Dolly said, "Ank u or oming." (Thank you for coming.)

Even though Dolly has experienced many challenges in life, it is obvious that Dolly's big smile and love have touched her many friends with happiness.

What about you? Have you shared any happiness today?

ABOUT THE AUTHOR

It is a joy for me to share this story with you. Our character is happy, she is loved, and she smiles and enjoys life in large and small ways. This is a personal story of love. Writing touches readers in different ways. As the author of this story, I trust it will speak positive responses in you.

ABOUT THE ILLUSTRATOR

As a native of Austria, Mrs. Dohm spent her youth finding lovely small wildflowers to paint. As an adult, she moved to the United States, married, raised three children, and finished her studies in Studio Art at Rockford College, Rockford, Illinois. She then began a long career in creating fine art and conducting painting workshops in Europe and the United States. She has also been the watercolor instructor on cruise ships. This is her first collaboration on a book.

www.ingramcontent.com/pod-product-compliance
Lightning Source LLC
Chambersburg PA
CBHW061226070526
44584CB00029B/4011